W9-AUI-874

# NOW

# I

KIDS
TELL KIDS
ABOUT
SAFETY

# KNOW

# BETTER

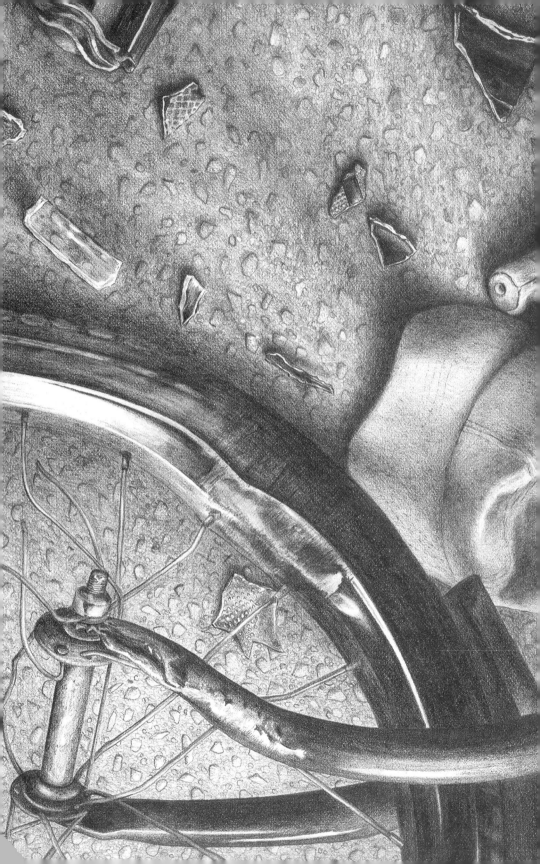

# NOW I KNOW BETTER

**KIDS TELL KIDS ABOUT SAFETY**

Pediatric Emergency Department
Children's Hospital at Yale-New Haven

The Millbrook Press
Brookfield, Connecticut

Now I know better : kids tell kids about safety / Children's Hospital
   at Yale-New Haven
               p.   cm.
       Includes bibliographical references and index.
       Summary: Young people ages five to nineteen describe accidents they
   have had, with their own safety advice and the comments of emergency
   room doctors.
       ISBN 0-7613-0109-7 (S&L). — ISBN 0-7613-0149-6 (trade)
       1. Children's accidents—Prevention—Juvenile literature.
   2. Safety education—Juvenile literature.  [1. Safety. 2. Children's writings
   3. Youths' writings.]  I. Children's Hospital at Yale-New Haven.
   HV675.5.N68 1996
   613.6—dc20          96-19411
               CIP
               AC

Published by Millbrook Press, Inc.
Brookfield, Connecticut

To pediatric emergency personnel everywhere
who do all they can to heal the hurts and prevent
them from happening.

# Contents

# Editor's Note

The preparation of this book hinged on the support of many. Vincent Conti, senior vice president with Yale-New Haven Hospital and the Children's Hospital at Yale-New Haven and Norman Siegel, MD, acting chief of pediatrics at the Children's Hospital and acting chairman of pediatrics at the Yale School of Medicine, created the environment that encouraged this undertaking. My physician colleagues provided invaluable advice, guidance, and inspiration. Youngsters needing emergency room services can find no better team than Jill Baren, MD; Jean Klig, MD; Veena Kumar, MD; and Erica Liebelt, MD. The assistance provided by Linda Degutis, DrPH, in identifying and compiling research data on pediatric injuries was a blessing, and her enthusiasm was a constant encouragement.

Reading 700 letters is an unusual challenge for those of us who are not schoolteachers. After extensive review and discussion, we selected 70 articles. The choices were difficult because some worthy stories had to be left out for lack of room.

Thanks to Mary Beth Esposito, RN; Donna Donovan, RN; Monica Joyce, RN; and Denine Baxter, RN, for their perceptive insights. Preparing the many drafts and details of the project would have been impossible without the support of Debra Nolan and Michele Mastropetre, as well as the assistance of Linda Wickett and Louise DiRuccio. Ken Best and Katie Krauss each brought a much-needed critical eye to this book. And to Tom Urtz, who had the idea for this project and had a vision of where we could go with it, extra special thanks.

Finally, thanks to Yale Preferred Health and American Medical Response for their support of this educational effort.

# Introduction

Every day my colleagues and I see injuries that could have been avoided, children in pain and parents in anguish. No one is more interested in preventing injuries than those of us who face these scenes on a daily basis.

As a group of us from the Children's Hospital talked about ways to share injury prevention messages with youngsters, one colleague noted that kids often pay more attention to other kids than they do to adults. So why not let kids be the teachers? We turned to children, and this book is the result.

The advice offered here is based on the experiences of kids from ages 5 to 19, and it is told in their own words. We hope everyone who reads these personal accounts will understand the steps they need to take to protect themselves, their siblings, and their friends from similar accidents.

Thank you to the boys and girls who shared their "dumb mistakes" and "weird inspirations." This willingness to be candid gives *Now I Know Better* its spark. Thank you also to the teachers and parents who encouraged their youngsters to tell their stories.

Learning lessons is a major part of life. Some, like the youngsters in this book, learn firsthand from their own mistakes. For others, a few words of caution from someone who is trusted is enough. When you are done reading this book we hope you can say, "Now I know better," and you won't need a trip to the emergency room to drive the point home.

David Bachman, MD
*Director*
*Pediatric Emergency Department*
*Children's Hospital at Yale-New Haven*
*April 1996*

# Axes

## Slicing it too close

When I was 10 years old, an older lady who lives on my street asked if my brother and I wanted to cut down a few tree branches in her front yard, and we said yes. We decided to use two axes in our garage. One was new and the other was old. I was wearing my sandals that day and kept them on for the job. I was very careful because it was my first time using an ax. I had not thought of putting on proper footwear. It went excellently until my brother went home to get a drink and rest for a little while. After he left I continued for about five minutes. I was chopping a big branch and swung too hard. It went smoothly through the branch and right in my foot.

I rushed home and my grandmother brought me to the hospital. When we got there they took X-rays and said that I was very lucky. The ax had come one-eighth of an inch from my vein. It was very close. They gave me four stitches. I was really scared at first, but then I realized that after they put the novocaine in it, it didn't hurt. It was actually fun watching the doctor put the stitches in.

I learned that you should always wear proper footwear when you're using sharp tools, especially axes. I would advise you to have someone with you when you use an ax.

**Billy Alexander, 13**

**Doctors' Comments:**
*It might have been fun watching the doctor put the stitches in, but not enough fun to do this again!*

*Axes are dangerous even in the hands of an adult. Would a handsaw have worked? It can be dangerous too, but it's safer than an ax.*

*Cutting down tree limbs is always serious business. They fall fast and are surprisingly heavy.*

# Bees

## Do not disturb

On my ninth birthday, my grandfather, my cousins and I went for a hike in the woods. We were looking for a snake. My grandfather kept lifting up rocks and logs and looking under them. As he lifted one rock, a swarm of yellow jackets flew out. It was their nest. We all were frozen for a moment, which seemed like an hour, until my grandfather told us to run. Matt and I ran one way and left everyone else. My grandfather ran another way, thinking Kristen and Danny were following him. When he saw that they were not, he went back, grabbed them, and ran back out.

My mother and aunt are nurses, so they called 911 because my grandfather is highly allergic to bee stings. Matt, 9, was fine. He only got stung twice. Kristen, 6, was stung about seven times. I did not get stung at all. Danny, 3, was stung about 20 times and my grandfather was stung about 60 times. When the ambulance came, they took my grandfather and Danny to the hospital. Luckily, everyone ended up being fine. That year I got the most exciting, but scary, birthday present.

This accident could have been prevented if we were more aware of where the yellow jackets were. But I think it would have been pretty hard to prevent.

My grandfather was treated with epinephrine [a medication used to treat insect stings] and intravenous fluids for about four hours and went home with a pain medicine and a cream to stop the itching. Danny was just given a cream for itching. Danny was very young and was afraid to go outside my house for a long time. We all are very careful when we go for hikes because it is not fun when EMTs have to come to your house!

**Megan Buckley, 13**

**Doctors' Comments:**
*Last summer must have been a good year for bees because we saw more children with bee stings than ever before. Most people recover quickly from a bee sting. Some people like Megan's grandfather, however, can get very sick or die because they are allergic to bees.*

*Stay away from areas where you know there are a lot of bees and never do anything to aggravate their nest (like throwing rocks).*

*If you know someone has a bad allergy to bees and gets stung, get them medical attention right away. If someone in your family is allergic to bee stings, ask your parents if they have bee-sting medicine (such as epinephrine) in your house or car in case of an emergency.*

# Bicycles

## Good reasons to wear a helmet

I was about 7 years old, riding my neon Huffy bicycle down a steep hill, when suddenly my shoelace became loose, but I didn't know it.

My shoelace got caught in the back spokes, and I crashed. At the time, I never wore my helmet. I was not alerted that my skull got broken. I saw lots of blood on my legs. Blood was coming out of all of my cuts and scratches. I couldn't even feel my legs. I went up to touch my head, as I seemed dizzy. When my hand came down, it was full of blood.

When I knew my head was bleeding, I really thought I wouldn't live. Fear overcame me. But after about five minutes my old neighbors, the Rosens, heard my crying and yelling. Mr. Rosen rushed over to my side, and the first thing he saw was all the bleeding. Mr. Rosen called to his wife and told her to call an ambulance.

After about ten minutes, an ambulance came to get me. By then, Mr. Rosen's wife got blankets for me and also supplied pressure on my head most of all. In the ambulance, the paramedics gave me oxygen and some bandages. When I got to the emergency room I was able to see the doctor right away. He told my parents and me that the only serious thing was that I had a minor fracture in my skull plus I would require a couple of stitches. I was relieved.

My message to kids is to always wear your helmet when you're riding your bicycle.

**Brenton Sutton, 12**

*the kid riding on the back or on the front handlebars who gets a foot caught in the spokes or the chain—and boom! Down they go. Wear shoes and don't ride double.*

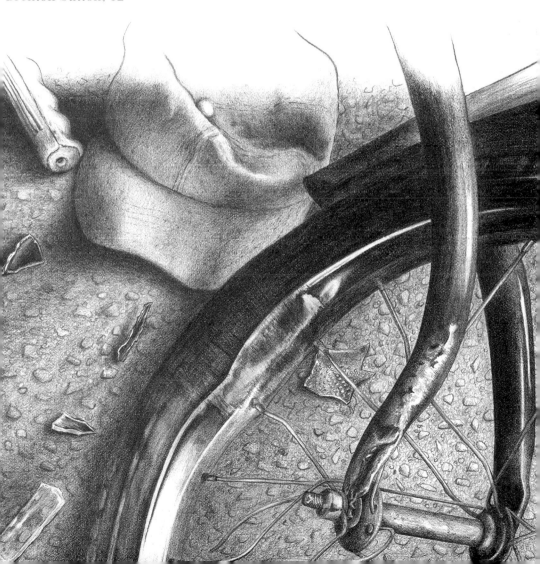

# Because I said so!

The summer before I entered middle school I went to my pediatrician for a routine physical. After my exam we talked briefly about my interests. I told him I enjoyed riding my bike. "Do you wear a helmet?" My answer was, "No." You see, I thought that only geeks wore bike helmets.

Two weeks later while riding my Red Line in my neighborhood I was struck by a pickup truck. I suffered a traumatic brain injury when my head hit the pavement and I was knocked unconscious. Someone called 911 and I was transported to the hospital. I can't remember any of that day and have to rely on other people to fill in the blanks for me. From that afternoon to three months later I lay in a very deep coma.

I suffered damage to the brain stem, which is the lower part of the brain that controls things like your temperature, ability to wake up, and even breathing. I was put on a machine that did my breathing for me, a tube in my nose fed me, and a bolt in my head kept track of the swelling. Day after day, unknown to me, my family sat praying and hoping for some sign of life. I was a mess and my family was not given much hope that I would survive. Well, I did survive, but not without a long hard fight.

With the help of dedicated doctors and therapists, little by little, I started to come around. I had to learn how to eat, drink, talk, walk, and even think all over again. I was confined to a wheelchair for months and had to endure painful therapy sessions both physically and emotionally. More than a half a year later I was finally able to return home to my family, in a wheelchair.

**Doctors' Comments:**
*The good news about biking over the last ten years is that the number of youngsters killed riding their bikes dropped by more than 25 percent. Nevertheless, 276 children under 15 were killed in 1994 and "failure to yield the right of way" was the most common reason reported by police.*

*Remember that you and your bike are no match for a car.*

*Good luck with your recovery, Austin. We're all rooting for you. And thanks for your tip. We think a lot of kids will start wearing their bike helmet every time— because you said so!*

I'm still fighting hard to get back to the way I was before. As a result of my accident I need special education classes. I still attend daily therapy sessions to work on getting my right arm and fingers to work. I need help getting dressed and need someone to tie my shoes. I am no longer able to play soccer or pitch another baseball game.

There are some things I can't remember, but I do know one thing for sure. If I am ever lucky enough to ride a bicycle again, I won't think twice about putting on a helmet. If I had been wearing a helmet that afternoon chances are my life would be a whole lot more normal today.

WHY WEAR A BIKE HELMET?...
BECAUSE I SAID SO!

**Austin Kamykowski, 12**

*Author's Note:* **My Mom helped me fill in the blanks and organize my thoughts.**

*Doctors' Note:* **When Austin woke up from his coma, his response to everything was, "Because I said so." A family friend put that saying and Austin's name on billboards and pins as a message to youngsters to wear their bike helmets.**

**Doctors' Comments:**
*Sarah, you had a big accident, not a little one. We're glad your dentist fixed you up almost like new. It isn't always possible. If you lose a tooth in an accident, dentists recommend the following:*

1. *Find the tooth. If it's a baby tooth, it doesn't need to be replanted;*

2. *Rinse any dirt off it but don't scrub hard with a toothbrush or anything else;*

3. *If the whole tooth was knocked out, have someone gently put it back in the hole it came from;*

4. *If that is not possible, put it in some milk or have a parent hold the tooth in his or her mouth under the tongue;*

5. *Go straight to a hospital or dentist. It's best to get medical attention within 30 minutes. After that, it becomes unlikely the tooth will survive even if re-implanted.*

# My broken smile

Last year I had a little accident. I was riding home on my bike in Rocky Neck State Park after going swimming with my sister. I had a bag with my towel in it, hanging on my handlebars, swinging near my front wheel. All of a sudden, I hit a bump and the bag swung right into the wheel! The bag got stuck, and the wheel couldn't turn. My bike stopped moving, and I flipped over and landed hard on the ground. The bike landed on top of me.

My sister helped me get up, while I was crying like crazy. My sister then told me to open my mouth. I did and she told me part of my tooth was missing! That made me cry even harder.

When we got home, I calmed down a little. Then my mom took me to the dentist. My dentist was very nice. He put a fake part of a tooth in my mouth where the other part was missing. Afterward I looked as normal as everyone else.

I learned a very important lesson. If you are riding a bike, and need to put some clothes in a bag, put them in a knapsack on your back so they won't go in your wheel.

If you do get into an accident like mine though, don't worry! The dentists are very nice. They will make your mouth look the same as it did before the accident. Whatever happens will be taken care of by people who care about you.

**Sarah Chatfield, 12**

# Who's goofy?

My friend was riding his bike on the city streets.
A car was coming behind him. So he took a turn
into someone's driveway without exactly looking at
where he was going and he hit the curb and flew
over the bike's handlebars. He was careless in not
wearing a helmet and he hit his head on the asphalt,
which resulted in a serious concussion. He had a lot
of experience cycling and thought he was the best.
He was rushed to the hospital in an ambulance. He
was treated and had to wear a bandage on his head
for about a week. My advice to everyone is to wear
a helmet and look slightly goofy rather than wear a
helmet of bandages that looks even worse. Be smart
and always wear a helmet when riding a bike.
Don't end up like my friend did.

**John Smeraglia, 17**

# Trouble on two wheels

One day in September last year, when I was riding
my bike, my bike got jammed up and my foot got
caught up in the bike chain. I was not wearing
sneakers, I was wearing sandals. My ankle got
sprained, and I had to wear a brace for a week.
Now a year later I have to wear an ankle brace
every time I play sports because many ligaments
are torn in my ankle, which won't heal for many
years. My accident could have been prevented if I
had only worn sneakers.

My advice to parents and their children is always
make sure you're dressed properly for bike riding,
or any fun activity, and always wear the proper

**Doctors' Comments:**
*We all agree with
John. Helmets don't
look goofy. Kids lying
on hospital stretchers
with lots of bandages
on their head look a
lot worse. Bad
concussions—and
deaths—can be
prevented if kids
would wear bicycle
helmets, even when
they are just riding
at home.*

shoes and a helmet every time you ride. I know I will!

**April Millo, 13**

## Slippery when wet

In March a person I know had a strange accident. He was finishing up his paper route and found himself in Vernon Circle. On some weird inspiration of his, he decided to ride down the hill as fast as he could. In the process of doing that and also due to the fact that the road was wet, he found himself unable to brake in time to avoid hitting a parked car.

After pulling himself together and feeling the painful twinge of broken bones, he got up. He picked up his bike that was twisted out of shape and headed home. Upon ariving at home, he explained his situation to his mother who drove him to the emergency room.

In the emergency room the doctor X-rayed his arm and discovered that he had broken his wrist and thumb. He was in an arm cast for six or seven weeks.

In the weeks to follow as he pondered his somewhat absurd predicament, he thought of the safety rules he should have followed. For one thing, he shouldn't have been going downhill so fast. Another thing, brakes don't work well when wet and slippery. Finally he realized common sense would have come in handy.

**Nick Freney, 14**

**Doctors' Comments:**
*Like Nick points out, all it takes to prevent most accidents is a bit of common sense. Kids and adults alike need to learn not to make decisions based on "weird inspirations." You need to ask, is this going to hurt you or someone else? You're right, Nick, there is not much common sense in riding down a wet and slippery hill as fast as you can.*

# Burns

## Playing with fire

Accidents happen, and some are more devastating than others.

A 10-year-old boy whose initials are K.B. was on a camping trip with his family and some of his friends. It was night, and they had a campfire going. K.B. and his friends were intent on making the campfire bigger; they threw sticks and leaves on it until it was a big as a bonfire. But to K.B. and his friends, it still wasn't big enough. In their search to find things to make the fire bigger they found a can of gasoline. The boys thought it would be the perfect thing to get the fire bigger. So K.B., standing about five feet away from the fire, took some gasoline and flicked it at the fire. The bonfire immediately blazed up, but when it did, it ignited the gasoline's air path, and K.B.'s clothes caught on fire. He immediately ran, and was burnt, until one of his friends caught up with him and threw a blanket at him to smother the flames.

K.B. was rushed to the hospital and was treated for second- and third-degree burns. Unfortunately, that wasn't enough, and K.B. died later of infection. K.B. died because he was playing with fire. The best advice would obviously be, don't play with fire!!! And obviously don't throw ignitable things (gasoline, hair spray, nail polish, bug spray, etc.) into the fire.

**Kendra Eckert, 13**

**Doctors' Comments:**
*Fire can be friend or foe. Many, many children die each year in our country from burns. In fact, fires and burns were recently reported as the second leading cause of death for children 14 and younger in this country.*

*K.B. obviously did something that was really unwise and he paid for it with his life. Please listen to Kendra. Leave fire alone! And what about your house? Do you have smoke detectors? Do they work? Does everyone in your family have an escape route?*

# Camping

## Not a happy camper

Asked to go camping for the first time, it seemed like a chance of a lifetime, not the end of one. I tied together a sleeping bag and packed my stuff in the truck. The three of us started on our way to the Berkshires. We hiked up a mountain for three hours in the pouring rain. I was shaking like a leaf when we set up the tent. I had not brought extra clothes. It was impossible to see three feet ahead of you in the fog.

Being unable to start a fire, I went to bed freezing cold, hungry, and wet. I would have given anything to be home. I began to panic. My body was too cold.

My mind chose to block out the rest of the night. The next thing I remember was waking up in the recovery room. I could not ask where I was because they had a respirator down my throat.

The doctor explained that I had fallen 200 feet off a cliff near the tent. A park ranger found me six hours later and called the rescue team. My broken body was transported to the hospital by Life Star helicopter. My temperature was 85 degrees, and my veins had all collapsed (an I.V. could not be started). My jaw was frozen shut.

When I arrived at the hospital my heart stopped, and CPR was necessary. My parents were contacted and told not to hurry to the hospital because I had no chance to live. The doctors told my parents if I did live I would be brain-dead.

Apparently I am not dead and have no brain damage. The hospital staff called me a miracle. I suffered two collapsed lungs, a ruptured bladder, upper and lower arms broken, and a shattered hip.

Now I assume that in the middle of the night, cold, hunger, and desperation sent me into panic and I left the tent for help. Preparation should have been thought about seriously—bringing warm clothes and adequate food. Also set up camp in designated areas especially not next to a cliff. If only I did these three things I would not be writing to you.

**Daniel Potter, 18**

**Doctors' Comments:**

*It sounds like a miracle to us, too, Daniel. You provide a vivid description of the dangers of the great outdoors. It appears you became hypothermic, which means your body temperature fell much lower than normal because you were wet and cold. When that happens, you can quickly become confused and disoriented.*

*Hypothermia is quite dangerous, and so is falling off a cliff! Whenever you are thinking of going camping, check the weather forecast, take adequate supplies, and camp in a safe spot. Make sure that someone knows where you are and when you'll be back. That way people can start to look for you very quickly if you do not return on time. Don't rely on miracles.*

# Cars

## Just do it!

Last year my friend Jessica was involved in a car accident. Her family was going on a vacation and they were in a rush to beat the traffic. Jessica forgot to put on her seatbelt. It was raining and the road was slippery. As the car switched lanes it skidded. Crash!!!

Jessica's car collided. She went through the windshield. At a hospital she was put into a neck brace, had stitches put over one eye, and a cast put on her leg. No one else in her family suffered much because they wore seatbelts. Jessica could have been killed and almost was. Now she has had her cast and stitches removed, but she still has to wear her neck brace, and it isn't pretty.

To all kids this message says to remember to wear your seatbelt. Wearing it should be a reflex, and if it isn't then make it one!

**Caitlyn Gleason, 11**

# Close call

Wearing your seatbelt can save your life. My mother's seatbelt saved hers. She was going to get my sister from an activity at school and slowed down to pull in the driveway. Even though she was careful, a man in a semi-tractor truck behind her wasn't. He looked away from the road for a moment too long. Before he could slam on the brakes, he hit my mother full force in the rear of her car and sent her and the car hurtling into oncoming traffic. As she skidded across Route 66, she rammed into a woman in a car coming from the opposite direction. Both cars were totaled.

Luckily both my mother and the other woman were wearing their seatbelts. If not, both of them probably would have broken their ribs on the steering wheel and had their faces thrust into the windshield. The bruises that my mother received where the seatbelt had been were a small price to pay considering the alternative. She also got whiplash and had to wear a neck brace for a while, but that was not too bad considering the circumstances.

If you ever think that it is okay to go without a seatbelt, think again. Consider the consequences. Accidents don't warn you that they are going to happen, so be prepared for anything. Prevent injury and save your life. Buckle up!

**Sarah Brown, 11**

**Doctors' Comments:**
*We treat children who have been in automobile accidents every day. In fact, motor vehicle crashes are the leading cause of death for children from 5 to 14 years old. When we hear an ambulance is bringing us someone from an auto accident, the first thing we want to know is whether or not the child was wearing a seatbelt or was in a car seat.*

*If the child was properly restrained, we are probably not going to find any serious injuries when we do our examination. If we hear the child was not properly restrained, we all cringe and hope for the best.*

Whew! glad I wore my seat

## Thanks, Mom!

Once upon a time there was a kid in a car whose mom was coming home from work. The kid wasn't even born yet. He was in his mom's belly. Suddenly another car flew across the road from the other direction. Both cars crashed and were blasted into smithereens. There were ambulances, police cars, fire engines...everybody! Luckily the two drivers were hardly hurt. Why weren't they dead? Because they were wearing their seatbelts! The kid was not hurt at all. So what does this teach you? Always wear your seatbelt. How do I know? Because that kid was me.

**Ricky B. Jones, 7**

# Choking

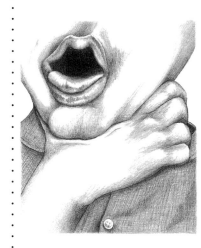

## A hard lesson

During the Christmas season my family received a gift basket from a friend. There were candies and an assortment of cheeses. My father gave my brother and me a piece of hard candy. At the time we were only 3½ years old, and it was our first time having a piece of hard candy. Our father told us to walk into the other room and sit down. Then as my brother was walking into the other room he started to choke. My father was able to dislodge the candy from my brother's throat.

The way you can prepare in case someone is choking is to know the Heimlich Maneuver. The Heimlich Maneuver is a way to help a choking person by forcing out the object that is stuck in the victim's windpipe. It is very important to perform this correctly because you can injure the person if it is not done properly. If you don't know how to perform this lifesaving procedure, you can always call 911. When you call 911 they will give you instructions on how to help a choking victim.

To prevent this from happening, never give a child under the age of 5 a piece of hard candy. Give your child small pieces of food. Tell your children not to run, jump, or lie down with a piece of food in their mouth. Make sure your children chew their food slowly and carefully. Everyone over the age of 12 should know ways to help a choking victim. I encourage everyone to take a first-aid course.

**Jennifer Federowicz, 13**

**Doctors' Comments:**
*When little things go into a child's mouth it can be dangerous, and food items are at the top of the list. Jennifer tells us about hard candies, but nuts, carrots, hot dogs, grapes, and other hard-to-chew foods should not be given to children under age 5 unless the food is first cut up into small pieces.*

*Learning the Heimlich Maneuver is good advice. As Jennifer says, if it's done properly, it can save a life. Other things to watch out for are balloons and small toy parts that young children can put in their mouths. They are dangerous, too.*

# Cuts

## Emergency room, this way

It all happened when my father and I were fixing a hole in the side of our roof. We were taking turns nailing in the sheet metal to cover up the hole when the phone rang. My dad went in the house to get the phone, and I kept on working. The ladder that I was working on was old, and it was on unstable ground. It is quite obvious what happened next. I fell. But in the split second when I was loosing my balance, my natural reflexes kicked in, and I grabbed for the roof; and instead, my hand slapped the sheet metal's open edge putting some major gashes in my hand. With blood all over me, I ran inside to hear my dad give the phone the usual, "No, I'm not interested in what you are selling" routine.

Taking one look at me, my parents made that gasping-hissing noise that parents do when they see their children hurt. Almost instantaneously they rushed me to the hospital. I was soon in the ER getting pain killers that made me very drowsy, and I was getting my hand stitched up. In all, I received 16 stitches and was equipped with a bottle of painkillers. For once I had a good excuse for not doing my homework on time.

This whole situation was caused by my laziness. All I had to do was get the better ladder from the backyard instead of settling for the old ladder in front. Also, to prevent such a thing from happening to your child, you could do a careful check of all equipment prior to use and make sure that our child is always careful. And if something like this does happen to you or your child, get treatment for it immediately to prevent prolonged pain and/or infection.

Marc Brooks, 13

## Kitchen casualty

Dinnertime. Mom was away, so it was up to me to make dinner. I opened the pantry and grabbed a can of soup. I opened the can and raised the lid. Suddenly, disaster struck. One moment, my finger was clean and unsevered, and then the next moment, there was a cut and blood was gushing out of my pinkie.

After I stopped panicking, I quickly washed the wound with soap and water. Then, a bandage and antibiotic were put on the wound. Luckily, that saved me from a trip to the hospital, lockjaw, or something even worse....

Of course, all that could have been avoided easily. (I don't mean skipping dinner.) If I had been watching the can and my finger, disaster could have been avoided. Luckily for me, nothing tragic happened. So, if you are opening a can, please watch your grubby little fingers, before they're suddenly covered with little red lines.

Alex Wang, 12

**Doctors' Comments:**
*Stories like Marc's are all too common. Be sure you have a stable ladder in good condition, and remind your brothers and sisters that tools and ladders aren't playthings.*

*We see a lot of "grubby little fingers" that get injured because they are in the wrong place at the wrong time. More and more kids are doing their own cooking when parents are at work, and it is important to be careful because a kitchen is a danger-ous place. Be sure to keep an eye on the grubby little fingers of your brothers and sisters, too, and don't let them grab hold of cans with sharp lids.*

# The truth...

My sister, January, came bursting through the back door crying one day. She told me she was climbing a tree and slipped. She said her foot somehow got cut open. When mom returned Jan told her the same story. Mom bandaged her foot and walked away. She wasn't too concerned about the foot because it was only a small cut. Little did she know that the small cut would cause big problems.

The next day January's foot was huge and very swollen. She was in so much pain that she couldn't stand it any more. She told mom what really happened. She said she'd been playing on an old woodpile and she had stepped on a rusty nail.

Mom called the doctor and took her to the emergency room immediately. When they got there the doctors said January's foot was infected and she had to be hospitalized, so Jan and Mom checked in.

After three weeks in the hospital January was very happy to come home. When she came home my mom, dad, and January had a long talk. They talked about the importance of listening to the rules they made and the problems caused by her carelessness. She missed way too much school. Mom missed work, and the hospital bills were enormous. If she had told the truth she would have gotten the right treatment, right away. So, the point of this paper is for kids to learn to listen to their parents and always play it safe. If you do get hurt, tell your parents exactly what happened. It makes a difference.

**Amanda Thompson, 13**

**Doctors' Comments:**
*Would January's foot have become infected if she went to the hospital when she first injured herself? We don't know. Even with the best of care sometimes puncture wounds still get infected.*

*Amanda's advice is on target. If you hurt yourself, you should tell your parents exactly what happened. In the emergency department a lot of what we do depends on what actually happened, so we need to hear the truth.*

# The whole truth...

Tom was sleeping over that day. My brother tried to reach for the cup in the cabinet, but he accidently dropped it on the floor and smashed it. My brother didn't want to get in trouble, so he asked me to help him and tell nobody. I gathered all the pieces, and put them in a plastic bag, so no pieces would fall out, and threw it in the garbage.

On garbage day my dad and Tom were taking out the trash. When Tom carried the garbage bag out, nothing happened. When he put the garbage down, some of the broken glass was sticking out of the bag. The glass cut him in the calf. You could see the meat inside of his calf. It was nasty. When my dad found out that Tom was cut, he ran inside the house, got the keys, and drove Tom to the hospital. The doctor stitched it up.

When someone in your house breaks a cup, dish, or anything that can be broken, tell your parents right away, don't do what I did. Let your parents clean it up. Remember, tell your parents to wrap it in newspaper and put it in 2 bags. Try to remind your dad that he has broken glass in the garbage bag and to keep the garbage bag away from his body.

**Sonee Pathammarang, 14**

**Doctors' Comments:**
*You are right, Sonee. Broken glass needs to be cleaned up carefully, and it is better to tell your parents up front, instead of waiting until something else bad happens. Tom's injury didn't need to happen.*

# Warning

I played outside with no shoes on, sliding on a slip-and-slide. It's a game. You connect a hose to a slide and you run and slip down, using your body, on the slide. As I was running, I got a big piece of glass in my foot! I was scared!!! I went to the hospital. The doctors gave me a shot using a needle. I cried. The doctors removed the glass and made me feel better. My Daddy and Mommy and Grandpa took me home. I say anyone who plays outside should wear shoes! No one should go to the hospital, like I did.

**Joseph Spacone, 5**

**Doctors' Comments:**
*It seems that in the summer almost every kid in New Haven comes to our emergency department to get stitches for a cut foot. Usually we spend five or ten minutes just washing off the foot because the child wasn't wearing shoes.*

*It doesn't matter where you live, there is always some glass, rocks, metal, or something else in the ground that can injure you. Always wear your shoes when you play outside. It beats spending a summer afternoon in a hospital emergency room.*

GLass in my Fo

Jose

# Dogs

## Not my best friend

I want to tell you about an incident that happened when I was 9 years old. One warm summer day my friend and I were collecting shells and rocks on the beach. My friend (we just met) wanted to show me a very big clamshell. He invited me to go to his trailer to see it.

As we got up to his trailer I saw a huge husky with grey and white colors. I had never seen the dog before so I wanted to pet him and look at him closely. I patted his head and asked if the dog was dangerous; then before my friend could answer the dog bit me in the arm. My friend pulled on the dog to get it away. The dog meant to get my face, but I put my arm in the way of it. I really didn't feel anything because I was in too much shock. Things were going through my mind—things like, "Am I going to die, does this dog have rabies, will my arm be okay?" The hospital was at least a half-hour drive, and as the minutes passed the pain grew.

I got at least 13 stitches in my arm and two drains to prevent infections. I had to get two prescription pills for pain.

The dog did not have rabies, and I wasn't the only person who was bit by it but I was the worst one. What I am saying is that you should never go up and pet strange animals. I had to learn it the hard way.

**Scott Vollono, 13**

**Doctors' Comments:**
*You sure did learn the hard way, Scott. Most dog bites are not caused by stray dogs; they're caused by family or neighbors' pets. We see many dog bites, particularly during the summer. Unfortunately, children are often bitten on the face and arms. Even with the help of our plastic surgeons, many end up with disfiguring scars.*

*Bites from many animals including dogs, raccoons, cats, and bats can also cause rabies. There is no cure for rabies, but fortunately there is preventative treatment that is very effective when someone is bitten. Be careful around dogs and never try to pet a wild animal.*

# Doors

## Crunch time

One afternoon my brother and I were going to the park to have our pictures taken for baseball. We both ran to the car and jumped in. As we were doing that, we were still talking to our friends, not paying any attention to what we were doing. I jumped in the front seat. My brother jumped in the back, still yelling to our friends. I slammed my door not realizing my brother's hand was in the door.

Within seconds there was screaming, and it seemed like it took forever to get my brother's fingers out of the door. My mother tried to open the door but she couldn't. She asked me to go to the other side of the car door to try to open it from the inside but I had locked it. I was so scared. We finally opened the door. It really seemed like forever.

My brother, believe it or not, was okay. His fingers were all there and not one finger was broken. He was real brave. I think I was more scared than he was. I sure learned a lesson here. To prevent this from happening again, everyone in our family asks if all hands are in before shutting the car door, or any other door for that matter. So please, before you close any car doors, look. It could have been a very bad accident. I am glad he is okay.

**Kelly Christoni, 11**

**Doctors' Comments:**
*Great advice, Kelly. Ask if all hands are in before shutting a car door. It's a simple solution that works. We've seen many bad finger injuries from slamming doors. We can fix many of the cuts and broken bones, but it is not much fun for us or the kids.*

One day, a little 3-year-old girl named Ezzy came home from the grocery store with the family. Her parents opened the van door to bring the groceries in the house. Her brother and Ezzy were still in the car. Ezzy's 7-year-old brother took her out of her car seat. Ezzy didn't notice that the door was still open. When she stepped back she fell out and cracked her head open.

Ezzy's parents came back to a screaming child. Her brother was stuffing her with Oreo cookies he got from a bag in the car. Her parents yelled at him because it's not good for you after you crack your head open.

Her parents had to rush her to the hospital to get about 20 stitches. They went back about three weeks later to get the stitches out. She felt much better.

To make sure this doesn't happen to you or your child, I would lock the doors and make sure you close the doors after you get out of the car.

**Catey Mascia, 11**

**Doctors' Comments:**
*Catey's story is not the first we've heard of a child falling out of an open car door. You have to be careful around cars even when they are parked. And Ezzy's parents were right. We don't recommend stuffing cookies in the mouth of a child who just had a head injury.*

# Drinking

## Lucky girl...this time

My friend just graduated from high school. She and a few of her friends decided to have a few drinks. I guess they got carried away and had a few too many. Well, she was unable to drive home, but that didn't stop her. She did.

You know that saying "Friends Don't Let Friends Drive Drunk." But when your friends are drunk too, that saying doesn't help. She and her friends got into the car, and tried to drive home. Even though they only lived a few streets away, she didn't make it home safely. Before she left her friend's street she crashed into a tree.

It was so late at night no one heard her crash. She wasn't wearing a seatbelt, and she was so out of it, she didn't think she hurt herself or the other people in the car. Then somehow she drove the car home. She and her friends didn't think they hit the tree that hard. They thought there was a little dent in the car. In the morning my friend complained about her knee and head hurting. It turns out she hit her head on the windshield, and her knee got banged up. We thought her head ached from drinking.

A couple of days later she was still complaining about her head and knee. Her mom took her to the hospital. It turned out she only bruised her head and knee. She was lucky. The doctors said she really could have hurt herself with a head injury. She says she's learned her lesson, but you never know. The car was totaled. Some little dent, huh?

**Doctors' Comments:**
*Allison's friend was pretty lucky. Every one of us in the Pediatric Emergency Department knows someone who was killed or badly injured because of drinking and driving. If you take a teenage driver, put him or her in a car at night when it is much harder to see, and add some alcohol, you end up with one thing: disaster.*

*Don't let your friends drive drunk. In fact, try to talk your friends out of drinking at all, or find some friends that don't drink. And don't ride with someone who is drunk. Otherwise the story of your ride home might have a much worse ending.*

How could the accident have been avoided?
One, if she weren't drinking; two, if she didn't drive
home; and three, she should have thought before
she acted. Also, she should have been wearing her
seatbelt no matter what condition she was in. It
could have helped her from hurting her head.
Because of what's happened to her I've learned that
drinking and driving is bad, painful, wrong, and
not worth it. Believe it or not she's actually lucky
to be alive.

**Allison Parks, 13**

# Drowning

## Turn your back for a second and...

I have witnessed an accident where a baby almost drowned. The mother was cleaning her bathroom with liquid tile cleaner. When she was finished she left it in a bucket near the corner of the bathtub. A while later she decided to give her 1-year-old a bath. Just as she was finishing, the telephone rang, and she left the baby unattended. As she ran to get the phone, the baby climbed out of the tub and fell into the bucket of liquid tile cleaner. By the time the mother got back, she found her child blue in the bucket. She brought her to the hospital. It turns out she was okay.

How to have avoided this accident: The mother first of all should have emptied the cleaner into the sink, and second of all, she should never have left her baby unattended.

**Alissa Belcourt, 12**

**Doctors' Comments:**
*Every year children drown in large buckets right at home. The story is usually just like the one Alissa tells us. Why? A toddler's head is so heavy that when the child looks into a bucket, it's easy for her to lose her balance and fall. A child who has fallen in usually isn't strong enough to get out. Just two inches of liquid in the bottom of a bucket can be deadly.*

# Electricity

## The electrifying experience

A crazy thing happened to me when I was 5 years old. It was a Friday, the last day of my first-grade school year, and I was so excited. All my classes went fine until I got to social studies. We were learning about our family tree and we had a sixth-grader in our class to help us. But when the teacher left the room we found out he was a troublemaker.

Then he dared me to put some scissors in the electric socket. Keep in mind I had a very large ego problem and I wanted to show him up, so dimwitted me accepted his bet. I took the scissors from him and without thinking I crammed the sharp scissors in the socket. There was no feeling at first, but then an electric current hit me like a rock. Luckily as soon as this happened I took them out. If I did not I would not have lived through it, and that is why I never take bets unless no harm can come to me.

**Chandler Moon, 13**

**Doctors' Comments:**
*You're right, Chandler, you were dimwitted...and lucky. The only person more dimwitted was the sixth-grader encouraging you to do something stupid. Electricity is serious business and worse if you're standing in or near water.*

*Don't stick things in electrical outlets or light sockets, or use hair dryers or other electrical equipment near water. And keep an eye on younger kids who don't know as much about the dangers of electricity as you do. If there are toddlers in the house, ask your parents to put caps on the electrical outlets.*

# Escalator

## Surprise attack

My mother was the person in my life who always warned me about accidents. Whenever I played around on the escalators she nagged me about being careful.

While at a mall with my mom and taking the escalator down to the first floor of a department store, she started to tell me about escalator safety. My mind wandered....

I was wearing a skirt that went past my ankles. I stepped onto the escalator, without looking where I was stepping. It was too late for me. Soon after I had gotten on the escalator, my skirt became caught in it. I fell forward, ripping my skirt, and tumbled down the second half of the escalator. Fortunately, there was no one else in front of me.

I was unconscious, had broken my left arm, and had a gash in the back of my head. My mother applied pressure to the gash in my head to stop the bleeding, while someone in the store called the ambulance. The ambulance would have taken too long to get to the mall, so my mom rushed me to the hospital. At the hospital, the doctor sewed the gash together, and put my arm in a cast. I knew that I was lucky....

Although falling down an escalator is probably not very common, it can be very dangerous. To prevent this accident, people using an escalator should always watch where they are going. Also, if you are

**Doctors' Comments:**
*Stacy, you are right that escalators can be very hazardous. We've heard other stories about a piece of clothing or pocket-book or chain getting caught in an escalator and the person getting injured. Think safety every time you step on an escalator and keep an eye on little kids getting on with you. Never let a child put a hand on the steps of an escalator because they can get caught, too, with horrible consequences.*

wearing long pants or a long skirt, you should raise it out of the way of the escalator.

Kids can easily get hurt. I was very fortunate to have a mother who warned me about particular accidents. I can only hope that kids will become more informed about accidents, and that every year fewer accidents occur.

**Stacy Winkler, 13**

# Eyes

## Getting the point

One sunny March day when I was 5 years old, I decided to play with my friend Michelle. We climbed onto the platform of my swing set and started to wrap the swing set up with string. When Michelle was cutting the leftover pieces of string, I stuck my head right up close to the scissors she was using. Michelle came to a taut piece of the string and cut it. The scissors jerked back and

**Doctors' Comments:**
*Young children should not be allowed to use scissors unsupervised and they should never have scissors with points. There are lots of scissors available for younger children that are very safe.*

*Most eye injuries are the result of industrial accidents or accidents like the one that happened to Bill. With proper protective eyeglasses or inexpensive goggles, most eye injuries could be prevented*

*Eyes are precious things. Close your eyes for a few minutes. Try to imagine what it is like to be blind. Prevention makes sense.*

poked me right in the eye. It didn't hurt much, but the vision in my left eye was blurry.

I don't remember much of what followed except that my Mom and Dad took me to St. Vincent Hospital where Dr. Mark Steckel did surgery on my eye. The scissors had punctured my eye badly. Dr. Steckel magically repaired it and gave me back my eyesight.

I learned not to put my eyes near any sharp objects and I would advise you to do the same.

**Christopher Alesevich, 10**

## Just close your eyes....

I know this guy named Bill who works at the Eli Whitney Museum. One day he was working on a wood project using a wood pick, a saw, and a hammer. All of a sudden he felt a sharp pain in his right eye. As the pain grew worse, the less he was able to see. A friend of his ended up driving him to the hospital, but it was too late. He found out it was a splinter in his eye. The doctors were unable to get it out. Now he is unable to see in his right eye and has to wear a black patch over it.

The advice I would give to all ages would be you are never too experienced to take precautions. Never work with hazardous equipment without protecting yourself with glasses or gloves!!

**Ilyssa Lish, 14**

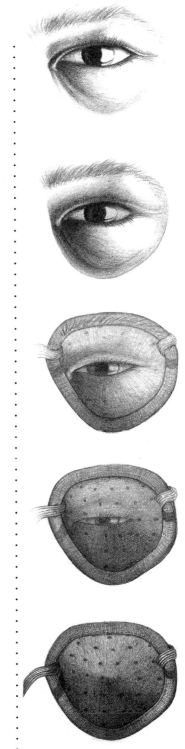

# Falls

## No more monkeys jumpin' on the bed!

My story is about a dumb mistake that could have been prevented. Everyone's mom has probably told them to stop jumping on the bed. Well, I didn't stop. I insisted she was being unfair, and I could do what I wanted.

It happened when I was at my friend's house. We were jumping on his bed when his mom came in and told us to stop. Ignoring her warning we continued jumping. Then I fell. Being only 4 at the time I thought nothing of it. Until the pain hit me like a ton of bricks.

I immediately started crying. My friend's mother thought it was just a bruise. Little did we know I had broken my collarbone.

It wasn't until Halloween that I realized I had broken it. When my mom was helping me with my costume she noticed a yellowish bruise near my shoulder. When she touched it I screamed with pain.

She immediately took me to the hospital. There I got X-rays that proved I had a fractured collarbone. The doctors put a brace on me. I had to wear that ugly thing for a long time! But that was too long ago for me to remember exactly how long.

The accident taught me one thing, never go against your parents' wishes. They speak from experience.

**Tara Cocchiarella, 11**

**Doctors' Comments:**
*Tara is right. Moms and dads all over the world try to teach their children not to jump on the bed. Some kids don't learn until they fall and hurt themselves. They don't learn until the pain hits them "like a ton of bricks." Tara only had a broken collarbone. She could have hurt her head, her neck, or something else that wouldn't heal as quickly. No more monkeys—or kids— jumping on the bed!*

## Crash landing

When I was 5 years old I fell out of a peach tree and broke my head. I was in a park and over cement! I had a bunch of rocks stuck in my head. My mom thought my back was broken. An ambulance and a police crew came. I went to the hospital. There, I had X-rays. The doctor took the rocks out of my head. I couldn't remember my cat's name. It took a week to heal. I think other kids shouldn't shake trees if other kids are in them.

**Nick R. Olsen, 8**

**Doctors' Comments:**
*After a head injury, some people never remember their cat's name and a lot of other things. You are right, Nick. If you see someone in a tree, don't start shaking it!*

## Off limits

I was playing outside with my cousins and friends. Everyone thought it would be fun to explore the unfinished building on the other side of the gate. I was the youngest and wanted to do what the bigger kids did. We all fit through a hole in the gate and ignored the "no trespassing" sign. There were many dangerous holes and pits everywhere.

We stayed out there until it became dark. We heard my mom calling for us, and everyone started running home. I began to run but slipped and fell in a hole. I hurt my knee and could not get out. I was scared and started screaming. My cousin heard me and ran back to get me out. She had to carry me all the way home.

After the accident I received treatment for my knee from my mother. My knee was scarred up bad, and I could not walk for a day. I heard a long lecture from my mom, and we all were grounded. I realized what we all did was dangerous and stupid. We took a very big risk ignoring that one sign.

After this accident I would encourage all kids to really be cautious and follow directions. They are not there to make you miserable. Parents should make sure their children are careful, understand the rules, and know the possible consequences if they don't follow them.

**Rhonda Newton, 17**

**Doctors' Comments:**
*Construction sites are dangerous places. We've seen some very bad injuries happen to children who play in construction sites. Signs are put up for good reasons—to keep people from getting hurt.*

# Mom makes a mistake

One Friday, my mother took the day off to clean the garage. Before she started, she did a load of wash. She couldn't reach the wash line outside, so she used a chair on the grass. Mom finished hanging the wash. She went to get down from the chair, and the chair tipped backward. Her pinkie got caught when the chair fell, and the chair bent her pinkie backward. One bone in her hand broke below her pinkie.

She didn't realize she broke her hand, so she waited until after supper to go to the emergency room. Mom got an X-ray of her hand.

When she came home, she was wearing a purple cast up to her elbow, and her arm was in a sling. Mom had to wear it for eight weeks. Eight weeks is a long time! That's two months with pain!

My mom gave some good advice for people who stand on chairs: "Don't stand on a chair!" It's very dangerous because you could fall and hurt yourself badly. Now she knows not to stand on a chair on the grass.

**Shannon Ford, 11**

**Doctors' Comments:**
*One of the hardest things about being a parent is teaching your children what is safe and what is not. We're sure Shannon's mom asked her many times not to climb on chairs or counters or too high up a tree because she didn't want Shannon to fall and get hurt.*

*The trouble is that it is sometimes hard for parents to remember their own advice. We're sure that Shannon and her mom think very carefully now about what they are doing before climbing on a chair or ladder. We all should.*

# Fights

## Oww! Why did you do that?

One day, I was at a friend's house with some of my other friends. I was sitting in a swivel chair. There was a boy who wanted to sit in the chair, but I wouldn't get up because I had just gotten in the chair. He started to pull my arm really hard. I told him to stop, but he didn't. Then I couldn't move my arm without it feeling like it was split in two.

We called my dad, who's a doctor. Meanwhile, my arm was put in a sling. Even if someone touched my arm it would hurt. When my dad got home he needed to pop my arm back into the socket, but it sounded to me like it would hurt a lot so I started to cry, but I knew if I didn't get my arm back in the socket it would hurt even more. So I let my dad pop my arm back into the socket. It hurt so much I thought my arm was going to fall off, but it didn't, of course. I took the sling off and relaxed.

To prevent this from happening don't let someone pull on your arm as hard as they can. And if they don't stop, then get an adult to help you.

**Emily Chessin, 11**

**Doctors' Comments:**
*We all have to learn to settle our disagreements peacefully. It is important, as Emily says, to get an adult to help when you find yourself having a disagreement and you might get hurt. The hardest thing to learn is to get up and walk away and avoid fights. If you walk away from a battle, you really have won rather than lost. And the next time you think about yanking hard on someone's arm, think again.*

While my parents and uncle were inside painting walls and tiling floors (my family was going to move into our new house in a couple of weeks and my parents were getting the house ready), my sister, Lindsey, and I were in the front playing on this really huge dirt pile. We decided we were going to make a house out of it. As I cleared some rocks in the "kitchen," Lindsey cleared some rocks in the "family room." I realized that wherever I moved, Lindsey threw rocks that way. I don't know what Lindsey was trying to prove, but she did do something...hit me in the head with a rock. It didn't hurt at all, it was the puddle of blood that was making me scream hysterically.

My mom freaked out at the sight of all the blood (which didn't help me). My dad and uncle cleansed my cut with ice. I was scared going to the hospital. But after Mr. Lockman told me there was nothing to be scared about, I felt a whole lot better. I felt better too since I knew his daughter from school. Mr. Lockman and my parents stayed with me the whole time. After I found out I didn't need stitches (whew!), I felt even more relieved. The doctors told me not to put pressure on my head and that was it. My advice to you is: Whether you're inside or outside, throwing things that you're not supposed to *could* cause the tiniest bit of damage. Oh! And don't be afraid to go to the hospital. Everyone is really nice.

**Stacey Oliveto, 11**

**Doctors' Comments:**
*We're with you, Stacey. What are kids trying to prove when they throw things, fight, or swing at each other with sticks? Someone always gets hurt. Yes, nice people will take good care of you in the hospital. But those of us who work in hospitals would be much happier if we had to take care of fewer kids who got injured from senseless fighting.*

# Fishing

## I'm hooked

On my summer vacation I was fishing on the shore on Cape Cod. I brought the pole behind my back to cast and when I pulled it forward the hook got stuck in my back. I tried to pull it out but the harder I tugged on my line the more it hurt and the deeper it went in.

An older man who saw the accident hurried over to help. He cut the barb on the hook with pliers, then pushed the hook through my skin to remove it. He then wiped the wound with alcohol, which made it sting, and covered it with a Band-Aid.

A good way to prevent this from happening again is to make sure my line is not too long, which is where I made my mistake in the first place.

I didn't let a hook in my back stop me from fishing again, but I did learn a good lesson.

**George Aniki, 11**

**Doctors' Comments:**

*Every summer we remove quite a few fish hooks from children. Those big blue fish hooks are the worst. One child actually got hooked through the lip, just like a fish. Another child got snagged in the eyelid.*

*You really need to pay attention when you are around people who are fishing. A few simple precautions could prevent some bad injuries.*

# Guns

## Real guns. Real tragedies.

One afternoon my cousin and his friend were playing cops and robbers. As they were playing, they came across a real gun they thought was a toy. They decided they would take turns playing with the gun.

My cousin was first to have his turn. He chased his friend around the house until he decided to scream "freeze" and shoot his friend. The boy fell to the ground as I walked into the room. My cousin dropped the gun as he ran over to him. I ran to get my aunt. My cousin and I had no idea what happened. We took the boy to the hospital, but it was too late; he was dead. For nights we had nightmares until we received therapy.

I was only 4 then, and I still know the proper usage of guns. My cousin is now in college and he's feeling a lot better about himself. What I am trying to tell you is that guns are bad; they are not something to take lightly. A bullet does not always hit the people or thing it was intended for; in other words, a bullet does not have a name on it.

**Senita Gillespie, 14**

**Doctors' Comments:**
*Like Senita and Tina say, if you see a gun laying around, call an adult. Don't touch it. Figure it's loaded and leave it alone. Be sure to keep other children from picking it up, too. Firearms kill more kids between 15 and 19 years old than anything else, even auto accidents. According to the most recent statistics, over 800 kids 14 and younger were killed by firearms this year.*

*With what we see in the emergency room, it's hard to understand people who claim they have to*

One day my uncle went to a grocery store and left his 5-year-old and 11-year-old sons in the car while he rushed in to buy what he was going to buy. Well, the two boys found my uncle's gun, which was under the seat in the car. It was way tucked in there, but they found it, and the gun was loaded.

They were curious and started to play around with it. The oldest one was holding the gun and pointing it around when we all heard a gun shot, which hit my younger cousin in the head.

They rushed my cousin to the hospital, but it was too late. He died on the way. This was a terrible way to learn to never leave loaded guns around. The 11-year-old is now almost in his 20's and still feels what happened was his fault.

The advice I give to all children and adults is never leave a gun around where a child can reach it. I think just never leave a loaded gun in a house, period. If you get your hands on a gun, never play with it. A gun is not a toy, it can take someone's life.

To the kids, if you see a gun laying around, loaded, call an adult to come and pick it up. Never, ever play with a loaded gun.

**Tina Garcia, 15**

*have a gun around the house to protect themselves. We read all too often of kids who injure or kill themselves when playing with guns or of parents who accidentally shoot their children because they mistake them for burglars. Senita and Tina know the tragedy guns can cause.*

*Parents, if you have a gun, keep a lock on the trigger, remove all the bullets, and lock the gun in a place where children can't get their hands on it.*

# Horses

# Too close for comfort

When I was 8 I went horseback riding with my father. Although I was quite inexperienced, I was riding an intermediate horse named B.J. I was riding western without a helmet. That's not a very smart idea.

My dad and I were waiting for our guide who was delayed with her own horse problem. My horse decided to bolt for no apparent reason. He was galloping up the hill, and I lost all control. I lost my left stirrup causing me to fall to the right, dangling by one stirrup.

As I was being dragged, I thought my life was over. I was looking down and I saw rocks and sticks flying by. I was crying and screaming, causing the horse to gallop on. I just couldn't stay on any longer, so I took the last bit of energy I had and kicked myself off the horse. I fell smack-dab on my wrist. It wasn't broken. I didn't hit my head.

When a horse goes back to the stable alone, the owners know something's wrong. Six people on horseback rushed down the hill to see what happened. They found me okay, but very scared and nervous. But I got the courage to get myself back on my guide's horse. After my accident, my parents said that if I wanted to ride, I had to take lessons. I agreed. I still take lessons and compete in shows. Now I always wear a helmet. After what happened to Christopher Reeve, I don't think I will ever ride without a helmet. Anyone who rides a horse should always wear a helmet.

**Julie Avallone, 13**

**Doctors' Comments:**
*When you fall off a horse, it is a long way to the ground. One of our doctors was thrown from a horse as a child. He was scared but he wasn't hurt. He wasn't wearing a helmet either because in those days no one thought of wearing helmets when riding bikes or horses. We all know better now.*

# Knives

## Ruining a good time

I was with my dad camping in the woods of New Hampshire. We just unpacked the jeep, and I had a big sharp knife. I was cutting off the bark of a twig. When whoosh, I cut my hand right by my thumb. I was shocked at what just happened! My blood was pouring out. I said, "Uh uh D-Dad." My dad came over with a towel and put it over my cut, as he applied pressure to my hand.

We quickly got into the jeep and drove to the hospital. I had to tell what happened and where I lived. The doctor had me go inside an examining room. But, was I scared! I did not know what was going to happen.

The doctor stopped the blood and put in three stitches in my hand. They put my nerves to sleep with a needle. The rest of the week was ruined. I couldn't go swimming or run around. Now I have a scar on my left hand.

I could have prevented my cut by not playing with a sharp object. I should have waited until I was older. I know that now.

**Blake Abbruscato, 12**

**Doctors' Comments:**
*Knives fascinate many people. But when you use one, there is so little margin for error. One little slip and you have a dangerous slice, an ugly scar, or worse. Most of us don't think about how easy it is to get hurt. Blake learned the hard way. Listen to his advice and be careful.*

*A knife is a tool, not a toy. Treat it with respect.*

# A slice of life

My accident happened for a silly reason. I was at my friend Jianna's house to sleep over for the night. Another friend of mine, Ryan, was also there, and we were having a great time. We went to the mall and then to eat. When we got home, Ryan, Jianna, and I decided to stay up and have fun! We talked and played games all night.

It was around 5:00 a.m. when Jianna got tired and told us if we got hungry there were waffles in the freezer. Ryan and I decided to stay up even though Jianna was asleep. That was where our troubles began! I was hungry so we went upstairs.

I got the waffles out of the freezer and I grabbed a knife to slit the box open. At the end of the knife was a little twist in the metal, which I didn't think anything of. I was cutting and being careless when the knife went through the seal and into a vein in my forearm. That gave me a bloody surprise. Ryan almost fainted at the sight of the blood. After my dad was called we waited and I panicked. I thought I was going to have to get my arm amputated.

When my dad arrived, we rushed to the emergency room and the doctor put stitches in my arm. It wasn't pleasant. Jianna slept through it all. This all could have been avoided if I had just used more sense and some scissors. Knives are bad news and so are stitches. You shouldn't play with knives because even cutting open a box can hurt a lot!

**Sarah Gudernatch, 12**

**Doctors' Comments:**
*You're right, Sarah, stitches are bad news. A simple thing like opening a box with a knife isn't always as easy as it seems. Before you grab a knife or a pair of scissors when you need to open a box, think about asking an adult to help. Protect your younger brothers and sisters from hurting themselves, too.*

# Lawn Mowers

## Cutting it close

It was the middle of summer when my cousin was about to cut her grass. Between her driveway and lawn there was an edge of concrete. What she did was turn on the lawn mower on the driveway. While it was running she lifted the front end of the mower and placed it on the grass. Then she went to lift up the rear part of the mower and, unfortunately, her foot was under it and the blade slit the front of all her right foot's toes. And the worst part was she was wearing sandals.

Unfortunately my other cousin was the only other person home. Although she could drive all she did was panic and my injured cousin kept saying "take me to the hospital." We finally decided to go to the hospital, and the doctor gave her about two stitches on each toe and wrapped each toe in bandages.

My advice to everyone who has or is going to use machinery with rotating parts is always have protection throughout your body and be aware of hazards. Never wear sandals or be barefoot while outside. Even when not cutting grass you never know if there is broken glass on the ground and being unaware you may lacerate yourself.

Steven Araujo, 15

**Doctors' Comments:**
*Wow! Talk about lucky. When we started reading your story we thought your cousin would lose a few toes, or worse. Some horrible accidents have been caused by lawn mowers. Usually, the person wasn't wearing proper shoes or was mowing wet grass. Sometimes the child was too young to be operating a lawn mower to begin with. Use lawn mowers with caution.*

# Motorcycles

## Dangerous lessons

My cousin Gary had just repaired his dirt bike and decided to take it for a test drive at the sand and gravel pit behind his house. The day before, the company who owns the lake decided to dig a 75-foot trench. There were no signs or flags stating that the hole was there. While Gary was riding in fourth gear going about 60 miles an hour, he went straight off the edge.

He hit the ground and instantly broke his back and his elbow. He lay there for four hours in a puddle of mud before his mother and father found him. They called 911, and soon a helicopter flew him to the nearest hospital. When they brought him in, his body temperature was 40 degrees. They put him under a heating blanket and then they gave him a CAT scan and found that he had crushed a vertebra and broken another. They operated on him an hour later. They put two metal rods in his back and took out the crushed vertebra. After the operation they said that he was paraplegic, or paralyzed from the waist down. He was then sent for rehabilitation. Every day he lifts weights, exercises, takes a shower, and learns how to take care of himself. His advice to me was that every time you ride somewhere, always check the area you are riding even if you had been there the day before.

**Kevin Walsh, 13**

**Doctors' Comments:**
*Sixty miles an hour in a sand and gravel pit! On a dirt bike?! Talk about a setup for disaster. As Kevin knows from his cousin Gary's experience, doctors aren't too bad at fixing a lot of things, but they can't fix a spinal cord, or the brain for that matter, once it's been badly injured. Gary won't ride a dirt bike ever again. Mixing poor judgment with things that go fast can have tragic consequences.*

## Too smart for his own good

When I was 12 I wasn't smart at all. My dad had a 250 cc dirt bike and it is *very* powerful. He showed me everything and all the safety buttons and power switch. I told him, "I know, I know," but I didn't. He told me I could get killed. My dad was on the back, "just in case," and I didn't listen to him. I put full gas and whipped out the clutch. The bike flew, and we were thrown off. My dad injured his good leg and I almost broke my knee. I also damaged the dirt bike. I was lucky I didn't kill us! My advice is to listen to directions. *Don't* say "I know" when you don't. Look what happened to me. Now I'm scared to *look* at the dirt bike and when I do I'm scared it might happen again. Don't forget. Listen to directions *real* good and think safety first!

**Brandon Wilcox, 12**

**Doctors' Comments:**
*We're not sure a 12-year-old should ever be driving a 250 cc dirt bike. It's just too powerful, especially when an overconfident adolescent is in the driver's seat.*

# Nose

## No one is laughing

When Karen was 3 she was just trying to show off for two other cousins when they were watching T.V. She took the leftover kernels from the bottom of the bowl of popcorn and stuck two kernels up her small nostrils. She kept them up there for about a minute and got a couple of laughs. Then she tried to take them out. She tried so hard her nostrils were as red as blood. She screamed at the top of her lungs to her mom. Her mom jammed the tweezers up her nose. Her family gave up, and they rushed her to the hospital while she was still losing air.

In the emergency room they had no idea how she got them in there. They held one side of her nostril and told her to blow. The doctors decided to stick the tweezers up her nose while she was pushing with her index fingers from the top to bottom. Finally the kernels popped out. She only has a couple of scars in her nostrils.

I dearly suggest that you never stick popcorn kernels up your nose to be funny because it's a serious accident.

**Dan Strang, 12**

**Doctors' Comments:**
*You can't believe all the different objects we've have taken out of kids' noses and ears. Peanuts, pennies, beads, toys, and pieces of food, to name just a few. Most of the time the kid was fooling around, playing a game, or trying to be cute. When you think about it, there is really nothing funny about a popcorn kernel in your nose. When it comes time to have it removed, no one will be laughing.*

# Pedestrians

## Mean streets

One day a couple of my friends and I were walking down Dixwell Avenue and my friend Lorenzo said, "Bet you that I'll get across the street before this car comes."

He started running. BOOM! He got hit. He flew about ten stories high and came back down and broke a leg. His legs were twisted. They were dripping with blood, and we told someone to call the ambulance and get his grandmother. He got a cast on his leg and crutches, and the cast had bars through it to hold his bone straight. My advice is, don't go running across the street. Look both ways and don't make a dangerous bet.

**Carmella Suggs, 13**

**Doctors' Comments:**
*All we can say is BOOM! Wake up and think straight. Cross at the crosswalk, not in the middle of the block. In one year, 84 percent of the young pedestrians struck by cars and killed were not in a crosswalk when they were hit.*

*When one member of our team walked into his college dormitory at the start of the school year, he was greeted with a sign that said, "Life is tough, but it's tougher when you are stupid." Lorenzo should understand what that means.*

# The price of impatience

It all started when my younger sister Kristy and I were walking home from school. My best friend, Jessica, who was with us suggested that we should go over to her house and play.

We got to the point where mom usually waits for us, because of the heavy traffic on the street. Mom always crosses us. Mom wasn't there yet so Kristy decided she would cross by herself. When she was halfway across the street, a speeding car came down from the left side of the street. Kristy froze when she saw the car, and it hit her and she flew over its roof. When she hit the ground I ran over to her. She looked at me, then closed her eyes.

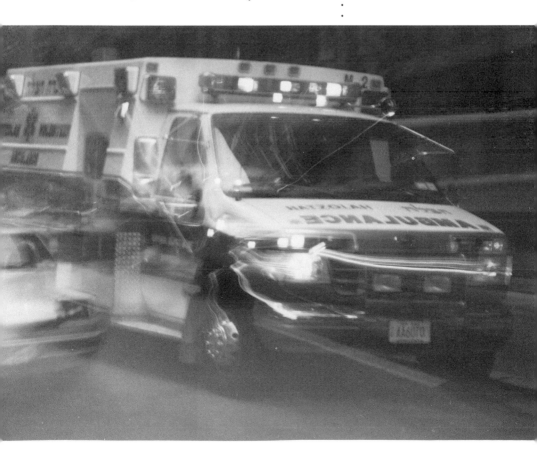

My mom and Jessica's mom saw the accident and called for the ambulance. I stayed with Kristy until a man pulled me away. He said the medical people need room to take care of Kristy. Then my mom ran out crying and shrieking. Kristy kept calling my name. I called back to her. Everyone kept crowding around her. Finally I couldn't see her at all. Her shrieks were mixed with my mother's. I stood there frozen. They put her in the ambulance and I watched it drive down the road. I began to cry.

Kristy only had a broken leg. She had to have surgery and two pins put into her leg from the accident. The doctor said she is fine. You wouldn't have known she had ever been in an accident.

This never would have happened if Kristy had waited for my mom like we did every other day. You should always listen to your parents because they are usually right. Mom told us before that we should never cross that road without her supervision. She was right!

**Laura Lee Kirk, 11**

# Unhappy ending

It started on a beautiful sunny morning. My older brother Danny (10), my younger brother Peter (4), and I (7) were outside with our neighbors across the street reading a book. My mom just finished making a batch of cookies and was outside in her garden. A couple of times Peter asked us to cross him over the street to our house to get some cookies, so we did. After a while I stepped into the house to put the book away and I heard these car wheels skid. I looked outside and I saw Peter twirling in the air, and then his head and body hitting the curb. I ran out to the backyard where my mom and dad were and told them Peter was hit by a car. They ran out front and told me to call 911. The ambulance came and took Peter to the hospital.

It might have been only three hours but it felt like seven. I kept on thinking and hoping Peter was okay, but I had this deep dark feeling he wasn't. Then a nurse came and told us that he had died, and suddenly I felt a sharp pain in my heart.

After the accident I kept on thinking, "If only I had kept a better eye on him or told him to ask me to cross him over," but it was too late.

My advice to anyone with a child is to never leave him/her near the road. Teach them to look both ways while crossing the street or to ask an adult to cross them because taking the time to teach them to look both ways could save their lives.

**Zoe Glaras, 13**

**Doctors' Comments:**
*Thank you for sharing your painful story, Zoe.*

*In one year, nearly 30,000 youngsters under 15 years old were struck by a motor vehicle and injured, and over 750 of those children died. Young children should not cross busy streets by themselves. Older kids should always cross at a crosswalk or intersection.*

# Blind spot

My name is Carol Greene and I'm going to tell you about an accident I saw. One day a boy was walking home as he was counting his money. When he was about to cross the street he dropped his money. He picked up his money off the street. But one of his quarters rolled under a school bus so he crawled under the bus. The bus driver returned and started the bus. He did not realize the boy was under the bus. The young boy was run over. Everyone ran over to him. Someone called an ambulance. He's dead now.

I learned that you shouldn't run in front of buses. You should not go under buses for any reason. You should let the bus pass first then you can get what you want. Also, you should go at least 10 feet ahead of a bus when you cross the street.

**Carol Greene, 11**

**Doctors' Comments:**
*Even when a bus has lots of mirrors, there can be blind spots, and it can be difficult for the driver to see someone who is standing too close. How can you expect the driver to see somebody who is underneath the bus?*

*Listen to Carol and stay away from the bus. If something falls under it, ask the driver to help you get it.*

# Playground

## Rotten trick

"Call an ambulance!" shouted the lady. I was on an overnight in the mountains with my camp. Some kids went boating while others were playing ball in the baseball field. Next to the field Mendy S. and his cousin (both 10) were playing on a seesaw together. They were going up and down gracefully. All of a sudden Mendy's cousin jumped off without telling him. Mendy went flying off and landed on concrete. He started screaming and crying. A lady quickly rushed over to Mendy. Mendy's arm looked bad. It stuck out one foot! Luckily the lady was a nurse so she knew how to comfort him!

Within five minutes an ambulance came. Mendy went to the hospital, and we were all scared. Mendy got a cast, and thankfully he was feeling better. Mendy went home from camp the next day, and he missed the remainder of camp fun.

This accident could have been prevented if Mendy's cousin hadn't jumped off the seesaw. So remember, don't jump off your seesaw without telling your friend.

**Mendy Hecht, 11**

**Doctors' Comments:**
*Good point, Mendy. Try to stay away from playgrounds built on concrete or other hard surfaces. Stick to the ones with soft surfaces like sawdust or wood chips. Then if you fall, it probably won't hurt so much.*

# Poison

## A real eye-opener

When I was 7, my friend Eric and I were outside playing pirates and searching for treasures. We found a small can on the ground, and I thought it was hair glitter. I took this can and I sprayed it on a tree in the woods. Eric was with me. The spray backfired off the tree and into my eyes. Then Eric took the spray and sprayed it too.

All of a sudden my eyes started burning bad. I was crying. Eric took me like a good friend and brought me to my apartment. I was screaming and crying. Then Eric's eyes started burning, too.

My mother and his mother found the can, and they said it was the mailman's pepper spray. They took us both and put us in the bathtub and gave us wet washcloths for our faces and eyes. We were still hurting for over one hour. It took a long time for the burning to stop. My mother called the poison control center to find out what to do. They told her that if we still had any burning to bring us to the hospital. But the burning finally stopped.

My advice for other kids is never to pick up anything they find that they don't know about, because it may be poison or something that could hurt you really bad. I know I will never do that again and I'm glad I'm not a bad dog.

**Jason Flores, 9**

**Doctors' Comments:**
*It happens all the time. A kid finds a bottle or can outside, and natural curiosity leads the youngster to play with it. Too often the kid suffers, and for no good reason. Jason is right. Don't pick stuff up if you don't know what it is. Get some help from an adult or just stay away from it. And do you know where to find the poison control center's number in an emergency?*

## Bad idea

I once ate poison berries. I was in my backyard and I was 3 years old. I didn't know better, so I tried the berries because they looked good. But they were poisonous. I said, "Mom, these berries are good," and my mom freaked out.

First she called poison control. Then she called my babysitter to ask her to drive the car because it's a half an hour away. She thought I was going to throw up in the car or die.

We drove fast to the hospital, and they were waiting for me in the emergency room. My dad came as fast as he could and said, "Do you want pipes down your throat or do you want to drink the charcoal the nurses brought to get rid of the poison berries?" I decided to drink the charcoal.

I had to take a sip every 12 seconds. It was a big cup. I felt very sick. I even threw up a lot. But I was okay. I had to wait in the waiting room for four hours because they didn't know if I was okay. I was worried, but it turned out all right. Then I went home.

The people in the hospital were very nice. They told me not to eat those berries again. "Don't worry, I won't," I said.

**Jacob Dilts, 7**

**Doctors' Comments:**
*Every year we treat quite a few children who eat pretty-looking berries, wild mushrooms, or seeds from flowers that grow outside. Salads and green vegetables are good for you. But unless it's growing in your own garden, don't eat it. It could be poison.*

# Just asking for trouble

One Friday I came home from school with a sore throat and a persistent cough. My mom heard me hacking away, so she brought out the cough syrup. At first, I was reluctant to take it, but after a while, I took the bottle to the kitchen and read the directions. It said to take two spoonfuls every three to four hours as needed.

Upon finding no warning on the bottle, I decided to drink some rather than measure out the prescribed amount. Tipping the bottle up, I took a couple of swallows. When I put the cough medicine away, I noticed that I had consumed a third of it. Thinking little of this, I went on my way.

Later that night, I started getting dizzy. Thinking I needed fresh air, I walked around outside for a while, but nothing would clear my head. Along with this, my breathing and heart rate increased. My skin turned clammy white, and my fingers began to tingle. It was at this point that my mother rushed me to the hospital.

Almost passing out, I staggered to the hospital bed. After almost an hour there, the reaction subsided, and I was allowed to go home with another important lesson under my belt. Always follow directions!

**Jesse Barton, 18**

**Doctors' Comments:**
*You need to follow instructions when you take medicine. Just because you can buy a medicine without a doctor's prescription doesn't mean it's safe. Many of them are quite hazardous if you take more than the recommended amounts. Even common medicine like aspirin can cause problems if not taken properly.*

*Younger kids should never take a medicine unless they get it from a parent or adult. Protect your younger brothers or sisters. Make sure the medicines in your house have safety caps and are out of reach.*

# Thirst quencher

Back when I was in first grade, I was the type of person that always got into things. One day I saw a milk container on the counter, and it looked like it had water in it. I decided to pour some and drink it. As I started to drink it, I immediately realized it wasn't water. I went to ask my mom what it was, and she said it was bleach. She made me gargle with water, and spit it out.

Then, I went to the hospital. The doctors in the emergency room made me gargle with milk. They told me that if it was any other kind besides the bleach my mom uses in the house it would have ruined my insides badly. The best thing was I didn't have to get anything painful at the hospital.

Now we label all bottles or containers if they're in a different bottle than usual. Of course, since I'm 13 years old I know what I can and can't drink. Therefore, something like this will never happen to me again.

**Anthony Dixon, 13**

**Doctors' Comments:**
*It happens year after year. Somebody stores bleach or antifreeze or another deadly poison in something like a milk container or a soda bottle. Then a kid gets hold of it, thinks it's milk or soda, and drinks it. The kid gets poisoned, his food pipe gets badly scarred, or something else very bad happens.*

*Don't ever store something in a container other than the one it originally came in. Keep poisons on the highest shelf possible or locked away where kids can't get hold of them.*

# One dumb dare

Have you ever had someone tell you that they are not allergic to poison ivy? Well, when I was little I believed that I couldn't catch it.

One day I was playing with some older neighborhood kids. They spotted some poison ivy and started saying how they had once had it and how terrible it was. Well, me trying to impress them and all, I spoke up and said that I couldn't catch it. They didn't believe me and told me to rub it up and down my arms. Since I believed that I couldn't catch it, I decided to go along with the dare.

BY: KATELYN MELINA

Never have I made a bigger mistake in my life. I came down with the worst poison ivy case! I had it on my hands, on my legs, on my stomach, back, chest, and face. It was between my toes and even in my ears. I looked like a big blister. I had poison ivy for one and a half months. I had to go for shots and use special cream for ages.

Now, seven years later I'm 13 turning 14 and still get poison ivy at that time of year. It's like a never-ending nightmare, just because I followed through with a dare that I thought I would win.

To have avoided this situation I should have never followed through with the dare. Also, even if you are not allergic to poison ivy when you're little or at any point in your life, it never means that you can't become allergic to it. It is very, very possible for that to happen.

**Katelyn Melina, 13**

**Doctors' Comments:**
*Listen to Katelyn. She's telling it to you straight. Just because you didn't get poison ivy one time when you brushed against it, doesn't mean that you won't get it the next. Don't go for the dare; don't end up with a never-ending nightmare like Katelyn's.*

# Skates

## I learned the hard way

Whoosh! I was going as fast as I could down the steep hill on roller blades.

Voom! I was gaining speed. I was not wearing a helmet, but I did not think anything would happen. I was wrong. There was a turn in the sidewalk and then a big bump. I went head over heels and landed on my hands, knees, and stomach. I slid to a halt. It seemed like every part of my body was sore. My knees, right elbow, and hand were bleeding. Somehow I had to try to get home. Believe me, you do not want to go up a hill alone, on roller blades, in my condition.

Once I painfully got up the hill, yet another ob-stacle stood in my way—disinfectant. My body was sore enough anyway, but now, peroxide? It was necessary though, or else my cuts might have gotten infected, and that would have been even worse! After disinfecting and thoroughly cleaning my cuts, I applied bandages.

My advice to you is go roller-blading with a buddy and do not go too fast down a hill. Most roller blades do not come equipped with proper brake pads. ALWAYS WEAR A HELMET! You should also wear knee and elbow pads. My injuries could have been a lot more serious. I learned my lesson the hard way.

**David Desjardins, 11**

**Doctors' Comments:**
*Whoosh! Voom! Crash!*

*Maybe that warning should be on the box when you buy in-line skates. One of our doctors skates, and he knows how fast you can go and how easy it is to fall. He wears a helmet, knee pads, wrist pads, and elbow pads. Now that you've learned your lesson, we bet you do too, David.*

# Skating to the doctor

School had just let out for spring vacation, and I was roller-skating with my friend Katherine. We were both very good, and thought knee pads and elbow pads were a waste of time. After we had been skating for a while, Katherine decided to get some cookies. She went inside, and to ease the boredom, I was pushing myself from rail to rail on her porch.

I heard her footsteps returning and turned my head to talk to her. I missed the rail, and my hand reached out frantically to empty air. My right arm flew out to break my fall, and I fell against the grey cement step. I screamed, and screamed again. Katherine and her mother came running and asked me if I could move my arm. I tried, but the pain was unbearable.

I ran home and doused myself with painkiller, keeping my arm in a sling until my mother came home. Although she suspected I might be overreacting to a bruise, she took me to the emergency room where after lengthy X-rays and false alarms ("It's just a bruise, go home," etc.) they detected a hairline fracture in the right radius, near the wrist. My arm was in a sling for the following six weeks, and I lost my writing and drawing ability for the duration of my injury.

Had I been wearing protective padding, this accident would not have happened. It was a pointless injury, considering how easily it could have been prevented, and the pain, the stress, and the money that could have been saved if I had been careful enough to take 5 minutes to wear wrist guards.

**Margaret Pritchard, 13**

**Doctors' Comments:** *Five minutes...that's all Margaret says it would have taken to prevent a trip to the emergency room. What she got was six weeks in a cast, plus all the pain, stress, and expense.*

# How I smashed my face

On Columbus Day, I invited my friend over. My mom said we could go to the park with her, and we brought our roller blades. When we got there my mom said to put my helmet on, but my friend didn't have one. When my mom left to play tennis, I first put on my helmet, then a few minutes later I took it off. My friend wanted to race so I said, "Okay." We were going so fast that I almost hit a bench, but I turned instead. I hit a metal fence and hit my face right into it. I cried, "I want to go home. I want to go home." My mom rushed towards me and I said, "My nose hurts." I spit out blood. Then my mom said that I was cut in my mouth, so we went to the water fountain to rinse out, and then I felt a huge bump on my head.

My friend was shocked. We got into the car, and my mom decided to go to the doctor's. We were glad she was there. She checked me out, and I was fine, but she said I looked ugly! My nose was sprained. I had a huge bump on my forehead. That night my mom slept with me. She had to check on me during the middle of the night. The next morning I went to the dentist to see if my gum and tooth were all right. They had to take X-rays on my mouth. I was all right. The worst thing was I had to go to school looking ugly. No one made fun of me, but a lot of people asked me what was wrong.

I told my mom that she didn't have to tell me what I did wrong. I should have had my helmet on no matter how it looked on me. So listen to your parents! They are experienced.

**Kristen Kelly, 10**

**Doctors' Comments:**
*Okay, so you put on your in-line skates and your helmet. Good so far. Then you take off your helmet and have a race. Not smart! Whenever you're on skates, wear your helmet, wrist guards, and other protective equipment.*

# Sledding

## Dashing through the snow

One December afternoon my little sister Alexa and I decided to go sledding. We took out our sled and put it on our snow-covered backyard hill, which had a thin layer of ice on it.

My sister jumped on the front and I jumped in behind her. We whizzed down the hill. We felt like we were going faster than a bobsled as we passed my stick trail markers. Then things started to get scary. We were out of control like daredevil riders. My sister started screaming when I couldn't stop the sled. When we went down a hill into some woods, I got flung off and hit a tree. My sister kept going and crashed into a concrete block, head first.

I got up and realized I was still alive. I saw my sister by the concrete block and she had a big black-and-blue mark forming on her forehead. I helped her up to the house. Afterward, my mom brought her to the doctor's office to check if she had a concussion. Fortunately, except for two black eyes and a big bump on her forehead, she was all right.

This accident could have been prevented by checking for hazards like concrete blocks and trees. Then we would have known not to use that trail. Another way is not to go sledding when it's icy. But that would be no fun. So I guess you could wear a helmet like a bobsled team. Remember: "Safety First."

**Tyler Combelic, 11**

## Headache #911

I once had an accident and I had to go to the
hospital too. I did a dumb thing, and I paid for it.

It was a cold winter day, and I was all set—
snowsuit, mittens, warm hat—everything. My dad,
my brother, and I were going to go sledding on this
huge hill right across from a high school. It was the
best place to go sledding. It was really long, and
you could go really fast.

My dad decided to sit in front, my brother in the
middle, and I stood up on the back kind of leaning

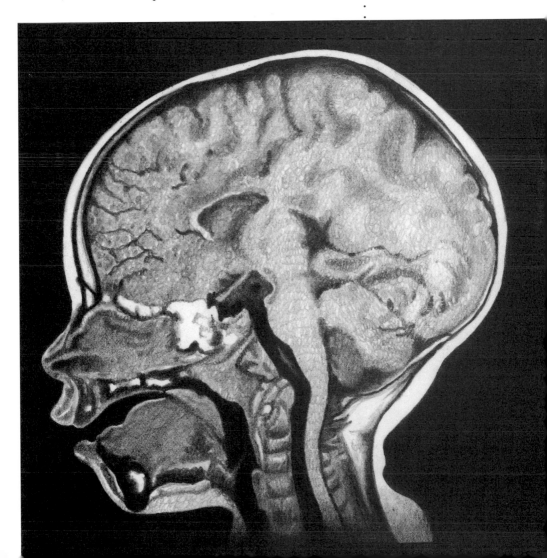

my arms on my brother's back. We pushed off and were going super fast. As we dropped onto the pavement off of the curb, I flipped off the back and hit my head on the curb. It didn't hurt that much, so I got right back up and did it again, but this time I didn't hit my head.

As we were leaving, I didn't feel too good, but I didn't want to complain and didn't say anything. When I got home, I told my mom what had happened and that I felt like throwing up. I did and a lot too. After my seventh time, my head felt heavy, and I soon passed out. My mom called 911, and I was rushed to the emergency room.

When I woke up again, a nurse was right beside me, and she told me it was morning. My mom, dad, brother, and sister were also there. I had a shot of water while I was unconscious so that I wouldn't dry out. I also had all these tests done on me, like an X-ray, to see if I had any broken bones in my head. I had an MRI, which does the same thing as an X-ray, but is more accurate. I also had a CAT scan. The tests showed that I was all right, and I went home later that day.

My advice is to never do a dumb thing like I did, and don't do something if it's too dangerous, even if it looks like fun. Think about it before you're going to do something, and if you think it's safe, still try to be careful, because it might look safe, but is dangerous.

**David Feldman, 12**

**Doctors' Comments:**
*Every kid seems to look for the biggest hill to go sledding. But you have to have some rules. Never put too many people on the sled. Anyone who falls off can get really hurt. Don't sled where there are trees, fences, poles, or big rocks. And like David said, never sled where there is a chance you will wind up going into a road.*

# Sports

## Injury time out

Once I broke my collarbone playing football. I was in a drill called sideline tackling. I tried to tackle someone and when I did, he got up and rolled over me. The reason it broke is because my shoulder pads were loose. If I was more careful and made sure all my equipment was tight, I'd never have broken my collarbone. So if you're a football player and you're doing a drill like that or in any football drill you do, make sure everything is on tight and in the right place. You'll avoid accidents, like what happened to me.

**Billy Manion, 9**

**Doctors' Comments:**
*You're right, Billy. It's hard for your protective equipment to work if you don't use it properly. Whatever sport you play, please wear proper equipment and make sure it is on correctly. And when tackling someone in football, do it the right way. Use your arms, not your head.*

# The crack of the bat

I was outside playing with my sister and some of my friends. My sister was about 8 years old, and I was 13. In front of my yard there was a metal baseball bat and baseball laying on the ground. So my friends decided to pick up the ball and throw it around.

Then my friend Nicole picked up the baseball bat and was swinging it around. Not knowing my sister was standing right next to her, she hit my sister in front of her head. I immediately ran to her. My sister was laying on the ground knocked out for about a minute.

My father did not know what was going on so I ran inside and got him. About a minute later her head started to swell up. We rushed her to the hospital. The doctor looked at her head, asked her questions, and said she was going to be fine, except her eye was going to swell up.

Even though my sister was okay, you never know what could have happened. So when you're playing around children be careful, because accidents do happen!

Danielle Candela, 15

**Doctors' Comments:**
*Ouch! A baseball bat to the head? That had to be painful. Make sure the area is clear when swinging sports equipment, and keep your eyes open if someone else is swinging. If you are playing catch, make sure the other player is looking and is ready for your throw.*

## That's not what she meant

Once when I was about 3 I had an accident and here it is. It was late at night. My mom told me to hop up the stairs so I tried to hop up the stairs and I fell and had to get stitches.

I could have asked her what she meant.

**Hope Fleming, 8**

**Doctors' Comments:**
*Quite a few children get injured on stairs, usually because they're going up and down too fast, aren't looking where they are going, or trip over something left on the stairs. Be careful. And when you talk with young children, think about the instructions you give them. If you say to hop, fly, dive, or run, they just might do it.*

**Doctors' Comments:**
*Have untied shoes
gone out of style yet?
We hope so. Sounds
like Paul, and most of
the kids in his school,
learned a lesson. It's
especially important
to have your shoes
tied if you're walking
on stairs or running.*

*It's amazing how the
simplest little things
can prevent the
biggest problems.*

# Chain reaction

One day when I was walking up a Lincoln Middle
School flight of stairs I didn't notice that my shoes
were untied. As I was walking I came to a sudden
halt, then went sprawling forward into the stairs.
That started a chain reaction, and all of the students behind me fell, too. When we all got up, I had
a bruised knee and elbow. That taught me a lesson.
Always make sure your shoes are tied!

**Paul Rozanski, 11**

# Swimming

## Water hazards

One day in the summer my cousins went swimming in the ocean. They live in Hull, Massachusetts, which is right by the ocean.

It was August, and the waves were so large that it looked like there were monsters coming out of the water. They went in anyway. There was a strong undertow, but they were only going to go about up to their knees. The current and the waves were very strong. My cousin Caitlin was 11 years old. She got pulled under and couldn't get back up. Nikky and Jill were screaming for someone to come and help.

Two foreign exchange students from China were also swimming in the ocean. One came over to help. He pulled Caitlin up onto his surfboard. Then she got caught in a big wave and got pulled under again. She was under water for about two to three minutes. The student got her again and pulled her to shore.

When the student had to go back to China my aunt gave him one of these things that says "Hull" on it for his bravery. To this day my cousin is still terrified of the undertows and never goes in when there is one.

Never go in the ocean when the waves are big or there is an undertow. When you go in make sure there is an adult nearby or in the water with you.

**Erin Harney, 12**

**Doctors' Comments:**
*Too many young children drown in our oceans, lakes, and pools. You have to respect the power of water and big waves and the dangers they pose. Even adults are caught in the surf and drown on many occasions.*

*Good advice, Erin. Always swim at beaches with a lifeguard and don't swim alone. Have a friend with you. Younger kids should be with an adult.*

# Mom to the rescue, barely

One thing I have learned is you should never ever go near a pool when your parents or guardians are not home. That could be a big mistake!

I have learned from a friend's experience. He went to the side of the pool when his parents were not home. He fell in and got trapped under the cover. Luckily his mother got home a couple of seconds later. His mom heard the screaming and she ran up towards the pool. The screaming stopped. My friend was drowning. His mom saw the pool cover ruffled, and she jumped in only to find a drowning child. He had CPR and had to go to the hospital just to make sure he was all right.

**Kevin Ostrander, 11**

**Doctors' Comments:**
*Your friend was incredibly lucky, Kevin.*

*Stay away from pools unless you are with an adult. Keep young brothers and sisters away, and make sure your neighbors have fences around their pools. Another piece of advice: Take swimming lessons.*

# In over their heads

One day I was going swimming with my aunt, her kids, and my sister. When we got there we changed to our swimsuits and got into the water. We were in there for a while. One of my aunt's friends came in the water to help us learn to swim better. I got the hang of it and then I stopped to go in the deep end with my cousin and my sister. First I just circled around the pool. Then I went back to the deep end. Stupid me went into the deep end in the middle of the pool, and the pool was pretty deep in the center of the deep end. I could hardly keep my mouth out of the water. I backed up some. Them my cousin came in back of me and hopped on my back. I went under the water and couldn't get back up. I started waving my hands, and my cousin and my sister pulled me up.

I could have prevented that by not going to the deep end when I'm too short.

**Kelli Bray, 11**

One time my brother was at the New Haven Lawn Club. He was running on the diving board and he slipped. He hit his head on the concrete and was unconscious and rolled into the water. A lifeguard had to jump into the water and save him. To prevent this you should not run on the diving board.

**Jacob Kalb, 9**

**Doctors' Comments:**
*Horsing around next to a swimming pool is one of the dumbest things kids do. Running on a diving board? Jumping into deep water when you can't swim well? Not bright, folks. Diving into shallow water can land you in a wheelchair.*

*Jumping on someone's back in a pool when the water is over his or her head can cause that person to drown.*

*Respect water. It can kill you.*

# Walkers

## A reason to cry

One Valentine's Day when I was little, I was sitting in my highchair. My mom was helping one of my brothers with a Valentine's Day card. I was getting fidgety so my other brother put me in my walker. Since my mom thought I was in my highchair and was rushing to get my brother out the door and off to school, she left the gate open that was by the stairs. On the bottom of the stairs is a stone landing that leads to the door. In my walker I went down the stairs and flipped over.

After this happened, and while I was crying my head off, my mom and dad made sure I wasn't seriously hurt. They checked to see if I was bleeding, and I wasn't. They made sure I had no broken bones. I didn't. All I had were some bruises and a headache. I was lucky nothing too serious happened to me.

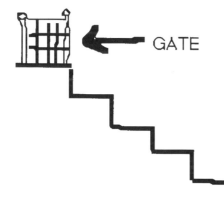

GATE

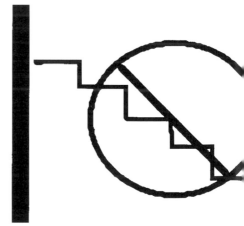

This kind of accident can be prevented by keeping the gates closed and locked at all times even when the baby is somewhere safe. You never know what could happen!

**Jessica Marchand, 12**

## They just aren't safe

This is a story that happened when my sister was not even 1 year old. We lived in apartments at the time and my sister was in a walker. My dad went into our cellar. My dad thought he shut the door, but he didn't. My sister went down the stairs in her walker. No one saw if she went down head first or not. My parents rushed my sister to the hospital. My dad ran three red lights. It was scary. I was only 4 years old when this happened. My sister ended up okay. After that incident my mom and dad bought a gate to put up in between the door and the stairs. Now my sister Melissa can't get down the stairs anymore. I hope that parents get a gate to put up or make sure the doors are shut tightly.

**Jessica Barnard, 11**

**Doctors' Comments:**
*The American Academy of Pediatrics warns people about hazardous toys, games, etc. The Academy does not recommend walkers. You can see why from the stories both Jessicas tell.*

*Mom or Dad looks away for an instant. Someone doesn't shut the gate, and the baby tumbles down a flight of stairs. Walkers don't really help children learn how to walk. Babies are much better off in a playpen or a piece of stationary equipment where they can play and practice standing.*

# Flashback

## A lesson never forgotten

I am not 19 years old or younger. I am 74 years old. I did not fall out of a treehouse, but I did fall out of a tree when I was about 10 or 11 years old. This is my story.

I came upon an apple tree that had one apple left on a branch. I could not reach this apple from the ground. Being small in size and weight, I decided to climb the tree to reach the apple that was at the end of a branch. I got to the limb that was holding the apple and I worked my way to the end of the limb to get the apple, and in doing so the limb under me started to bend. As I got closer and closer to the apple, the limb was bending more and more. Just as I made a grab for the apple, the limb gave out from under me and I went head first to the ground, chipping a tooth in the process. Except for my pride and stupidity, I was none the worse for my ordeal. I never did get the apple. In this case the accident could have been more serious. I could have broken my neck.

The moral of this story is, if you want an apple bad enough, wait until it falls to the ground—or go to a store and buy one.

**Aldo V. Guida, Sr., 74**

# Tips for safety

## from the staff of the Pediatric Emergency Department of the Children's Hospital at Yale-New Haven

### Basic Safety

1. Wear a helmet when you ride a bicycle or go skating. And never ride double with anyone.
2. Don't play with guns. If someone in your home has a gun, make sure it is locked away.
3. Always wear a seatbelt in a car. Never ride in the car when the driver has been drinking alcohol. And never drive a car if you have been drinking alcohol.
4. Don't eat or drink anything that doesn't have a label you can read and understand. Don't take medicine unless you get it from an adult. Make sure you know the phone number for the nearest poison center.
5. Look both ways before crossing the street. Cross only at intersections.
6. Don't swim alone. Be careful where you dive.
7. Wear the right kind of equipment to play sports.
8. Don't play with matches. Make sure there are working smoke detectors and fire extinguishers in your home. Have a family escape plan in case there is a fire in your home. If there are young children in your home, make sure there are no matches or lighters within their reach.
9. Be careful when you play outside. Don't climb on fences, handrails, or trees. And don't jump from playground equipment.
10. Use tools or machines only with adult supervision.

# Bicycle Safety

1. Always wear a helmet.
2. Look both ways before you start riding and after you stop.
3. Ride in a straight line.
4. Don't swerve.
5. Concentrate.
6. Ride with traffic.
7. Stop at stop signs.
8. Warn pedestrians that you are riding.
9. Brake and slow down before you turn.
10. Signal before turning.
11. Don't ride with anyone on the handlebars.
12. Listen for sounds.
13. Check out the bicycle before you ride. Make sure the brakes work and the tires are inflated properly.
14. Be sure you have the right shoes on—no sandals or bare feet.
15. Tuck in or roll up long pants so they won't get caught in the chain or wheels.
16. Keep loose strings or straps away from the wheels and chain.
17. When you get to an intersection, walk your bicycle across the street.

# Car Safety

1. Always wear a seatbelt.
2. Don't ride with someone who has been drinking alcohol.
3. Don't drive if you have been drinking alcohol.
4. Don't stick your head, hands, or feet out of the windows in a moving car.
5. Look before you close the car door.

## Sports Safety

1. Always wear the proper equipment when playing sports.
2. Warm up before you play.
3. Be alert during practice and warm-up time.
4. Know where the boundaries of the field are, especially walls or fences.

## Tips for Baby-sitters

1. Always be prepared for an emergency.
2. Be sure you have a phone number to reach the child's parents. Call for help if you have questions or a problem.
3. Don't open the door to strangers.
4. Never leave a child alone.
5. Don't give a child medicine or food unless parents say it is okay.

## Water Safety

1. Learn how to swim.
2. Don't swim alone. Make sure a lifeguard or another adult is watching.
3. Be careful where you dive. Jumping in is safer.
4. Always wear a life jacket when you are in a boat.
5. Be careful when you play near the ocean. Only swim in areas marked for swimming and swim only when a lifeguard is on duty.

# In case of emergency

1. Always stay calm.
2. Think about what you are doing.
3. If there is a fire, get out of the house and call for help.
4. When you call 911 for help, stay on the phone until the operator tells you to hang up.
5. If you are on fire, stop what you are doing, drop to the ground, and roll. (STOP, DROP, AND ROLL.)
6. If someone is not moving, talk to them. If they don't talk back, touch them and talk to them. If they still don't talk, call for help.

# Help and information

Emergency      911

Poison Control    _____

Your Doctor    _____

Your Dentist    _____

Neighbors, Baby-sitters, and other Adults    _____

_____

_____

_____

_____

_____

_____

_____

_____

**Credits**

*Editor*
David T. Bachman, MD

*Associate Editor*
Thomas M. Urtz

*Cover and Book Design*
Jeanne Criscola

*Cover Illustration*
Richie Hales Urtz

*Illustrations*
Richie Hales Urtz
pp. 12-13, 14-15, 22-23, 27, 28-29, 35, 43, 50-51, 56, 61, 70-71, 79

*Illustrations by Authors*
Christopher Alesevich, p. 42
Julie Avallone, p. 54
Jessica Marchand, p. 88
Hope Fleming, p. 83
Jason Flores, p. 69
Aldo V. Guida, Sr., p. 90
Austin Kamykowski, p. 17
Kristen Kelly, p. 77
Ricky B. Jones, p. 26
Katelyn Melina, p. 73
Nick R. Olsen, p. 45
Paul Rozanski, p. 84
Joseph Spacone, p. 32
Carmella Suggs, p. 62

Set in Bauer Bodoni and Folio.

*Visit the Web site for Yale-New Haven Hospital and the Children's Hospital at Yale-New Haven at* **http://www.med.yale.edu/ynhh/**

*Visit the Web site for The Millbrook Press at* **http://www.neca.com/mall/millbrook/**

DEC          1996

## DATE DUE

| | JUL 2 6 2000 | | |
|---|---|---|---|
| | Aug, 18, 00 | | |
| | | | |
| | | | |
| | | | |
| | | | |
| | | | |
| | | | |
| | | | |

GAYLORD M2